Old JEDBURGH

by
Judy Olsen

This picture was probably taken from the balcony of the Commercial Bank of Scotland in Exchange Street, looking across Market Place to the Canongate. At No. 9 Canongate is Halliburton's, a grocer and wine merchant's that was already at this address at the time of the 1881 national census. The premises are now occupied by an electrical shop. To the right is Jimmy Henderson's Temperance Hotel. The gap site was the result of a disastrous fire which destroyed No. 13 and No. 11 Canongate, formerly Beattie's the tailor's. No. 11 had been taken over by David Thomson's the draper's when the business moved from the High Street in about 1916. After the fire the site became Pinder's Cinema and afterwards was Walter Wilson's supermarket. Since the picture was taken in cold weather, it seems likely that the crowd is waiting for the Handba' players to assemble.

FURTHER READING

The books listed below were used by the author during her research. None of them are available from Stenlake Publishing. Those interested in finding out more are advised to contact their local bookshop or reference library.

The New Statistical Account of Scotland, Volume 111, 1845.

Ancrum – a backward look. Memories & reflections of Miss Margaret Kennedy JP About Bygone Times . . . , 1980/1981 (private publication in National Library of Scotland).

Smail's Guide to Jedburgh & Vicinity, 10th Ed., 1909.

Jedforest Historical Society, *A Historical Guide to Jedburgh*, 2000.

John H. Lewis and Gordon J. Ewart, *Jedburgh Abbey, the Architecture and Archaeology of a Border Abbey*, 1995.

Iain Mackenzie (ed.), *Jed-Forest Rugby Football Club – A Hundred Years at Riverside*, 1984.

Audrey Mitchell, *A Borders Schoolmaster, the Written Effects of William Lorrain A.M. 1772–1841*, 2000.

Scottish Borders Council, *Jedburgh Town Trail Guide*, 2000.

ACKNOWLEDGEMENTS

The author would like to thank the many local people who provided information and recollections including Mrs Carol Chisholm (Librarian), Mrs Annette Veitch (Registrar), Mr Alec Campbell, and Mr James Oliver of the Jedforest Historical Society. Special thanks to Mr Beaufort Robertson and Mrs Betty Robertson.

The publishers wish to thank Robert Grieves for providing the photographs on page 19.

The Edwardian mansion of Wells, about four miles south-west of Jedburgh, was the home of the Ushers, one of the wealthiest families in Britain. The postcard was sent in 1933, the year that Sir Robert Usher died. Sir Robert's grandfather founded the famous brewing and distilling business and his uncle, Andrew, donated the funds for Edinburgh's Usher Hall. According to George Tancred in *Rulewater and its People* (1907), the estate of Wells and Bedrule was sold at public auction and purchased by Sir Robert's father, John Usher of Norton, a Free Churchman and Liberal who transferred to the Unionists on the issue of Irish home rule and was created a baronet in 1899. When Sir John died in Cairo in 1904, Sir Robert decided to build a new house, which was under construction in 1906 when Tancred was writing his book. A series of misfortunes and the expiry of the family trust led to the gradual break-up of the 6,500 acre estate and the handling of the family's interests has become the subject of a long-running legal contest. The house was destroyed by dynamiting shortly after the Second World War.

INTRODUCTION

Most of the pictures in this book take us back to the early part of the last century, when newly-available picture postcards were used to send local news to family and friends. With the aid of the local newspaper, the *Jedburgh Gazette and Border Courier*, and the memories of local people, it has been possible to identify the exact moment some of these pictures were taken and to put names to many of the faces.

In those days Jedburgh was the focus of economic life for many surrounding farm communities and villages, and had plenty to offer by way of entertainment and social occasions. The summer events included the Jedburgh Games, as well as various outings and picnics by charabanc, railway or on foot. The new Public Hall in Abbey Place doubled as a cinema and in February the town's youth would turn out for a rowdy game of Handba'. There were political meetings, public lectures, and, of course, church, Sunday school and the Boys' Brigade. The men in the community could join the Ancient Order of Foresters, the Jedforest Instrumental Band, the Rifle Association, the Border Farm Servants Association, or perhaps take part in the running of the town. And then there was rugby, which has been played in Jedburgh for well over a century.

But what about the older history of the town? The origins of Jedburgh seem to date from at least the ninth century when Bishop Egred of Lindisfarne established the two settlements of 'Gedwearde' close to the Jed Water. Jedburgh Castle provided the early Scottish kings with a pleasant hunting lodge, but as one of the most important strategic sites in southern Scotland, it was often garrisoned by the English. Eventually the Scots realised that it was a liability and in 1409 it was systematically destroyed and the cost of this was defrayed by a hearth tax throughout Scotland. Jedburgh Abbey has survived, although the English attacks began just a few decades after the church was completed. The building is now in the care of Historic Scotland.

Jedburgh's strategic position also brought the town valuable trade. At various times different areas were designated for a horse market, a cattle market, a corn market and a butcher market, and farm workers and servants came to hiring fairs to find new employment. In 1603, when James VI united the Scottish and English crowns, trade began to improve, but after the 1707 parliamentary union Jedburgh found its tanning and malting industries hard hit by taxes.

By the end of the eighteenth century, improvements in agriculture and life expectancy led to an increase of population, high grain prices and unemployment. Many of those who could not find work moved to the cities or left Scotland altogether. In his 1834 contribution to the *New Statistical Account of Scotland*, the Reverend John Purves put the blame on the amalgamation of farms that had once supported five or six families, but emigration continued to take its toll on the community well into the twentieth century.

Attempts to introduce woollen manufacture got off to a slow start but by the 1830s the mills were employing hundreds of people. The map made by John Wood in 1823 and the Ordnance Survey map of 1898 both show extensive mill lades running parallel with the Jed from the Abbey Bridge to the Canongate, and behind the Bongate.

For a small town, Jedburgh has associations with a great many famous historic figures. Mary, Queen of Scots, visited the town in 1566, and nearly died there after her ride across country to visit the Earl of Bothwell. In November 1745 Bonnie Prince Charlie passed through during his attempt to win back the throne for the Stuarts. The astronomer and inventor James Veitch lived out at Inchbonny and the mathematician Mary Somerville (1781–1872) was born at her uncle's manse near the abbey, in the same year that the scientist Sir David Brewster was born in a house in the Canongate. Robert Burns visited the town and called the Jed 'a fine romantic little river', and the young Walter Scott made his first appearance as a defence lawyer at Jedburgh in 1793.

In the years before the Battle of Waterloo, Jedburgh was home to a small contingent of French prisoners of war who were billeted with local people and lived a reasonably normal life, tending gardens, teaching at the Grammar School, and working on building projects such as the new Council House of 1812. A hundred years later, in the high summer of 1914, the Jedburgh volunteers marched down to the railway station on their way to France as part of the British Expeditionary Force.

The photographs from the 1920s and 1930s show a tranquil country town, with familiar shops and streets. But although the lucky owners of the 1920s tourers and 1930s saloons were starting to learn about parking problems, motor accidents and speeding convictions, they could not have foreseen that in the 1970s a fast new trunk road would cut off the Canongate from its historic bridge and take a slice off the garden of Queen Mary's House.

In a way, the new road has also been kind to Jedburgh as there are no supermarket transporters thundering up the High Street. Many of the old shops are still remembered and one or two businesses are still run by the families who ran them a hundred years ago. Other than the banks and the Co-op supermarket, there are still no big brand names on Jedburgh's shopfronts. In 1834 Mr Purves observed that the town 'contains numerous handsome shops, in which all the necessaries, and most of the luxuries, of life can be readily procured.' This is still true today.

In 1910 the annual 'United Sunday School Picnic' for Jedburgh's children was held on Thursday 23 June and was attended by 741 children and teachers. After singing 'Onward Christian soldiers' they marched off to Allerley Well Park with the Boys' Brigade Band in the lead, followed by the Abbey Church School, Boston Church School, Baptist Church School, Blackfriars Church School, the Jed-Forest Instrumental Band and the Parish Church School. The children were given lemonade and pies and there was 'no lack of merry entertainment'. There were prizes for racing and wrestling and a medal and prizes for the five-a-side tug o' war, which was won by the parish church boys. Some of the prize winners are standing at the front of the crowd. The *Jedburgh Gazette* provided an exhaustive list of 'those present in the course of the afternoon', from farmers and shopkeepers to the Chief Constable: 'It was after seven o' clock when the children were called together, were marshalled under their respective banners, and marched to Market Place where they were grouped in good order at 7.30 p.m. and photographs were taken by Mr R. Jack, photo artist, New Bongate.'

Jedburgh High Street before the First World War, showing Smail's and Easton's printing offices alongside David Thomson's draper's shop. Thomson had previously been a draper's salesman, taking his horse and cart long distances over the Carter Bar and into England. The business moved to the Canongate around 1915, but later returned to the High Street. Thomas S. Smail took over his stationer's shop from his father Thomas, the publisher of *Smail's Jedburgh Almanac*, and *Jethart Worthies*, a collection of anecdotal stories about the town's characters in the early nineteenth century. As well as newspapers and periodicals, the Smails' shop sold a huge range of other items, including pens from MacNiven and Cameron Ltd., which carried the slogan: 'They come as a boon and a blessing to men/ The Pickwick, the Owl and the Waverley Pen'.

This view from the early 1950s shows the High Street looking south, towards Market Place. The main route to Newcastle still went through the town centre and the road sign between No. 17 and No. 15 shows the junction up ahead. The gable front of the library can be seen in the Castlegate in the distance. At this time the two shops at No. 19 were occupied by R.T. Russell, the tailor and outfitters. No. 21 was Brown's shoe shop and No. 23 was a branch of R.S. McColl's, the retail chain founded by Robert Smyth McColl – 'Toffee Bob' – who played for Queen's Park Rangers and for Newcastle United and was capped for Scotland thirteen times. All these shops have now changed hands, but Young's shoe shop at No. 7 High Street still occupies the same premises. The car outside the Spread Eagle Hotel is a Ford Consul.

In this view, probably from the 1920s or '30s, a bicycle has been propped up against No. 15 High Street which was Balfour's grocery shop and china saloon. The van stands in front of Main's the saddler at No. 17. Miss Michie (dressmaking and millinery) has Thomson's old shop at No. 14, next door to the fancy goods warehouse run by the Misses Fairbairn (note the protective papers in the window). No 10, which was Scott's the baker's until at least 1916, is occupied by Brotherston's which was in the same line of business – this is now Miller's fruit and vegetable shop. Further down the street, on the right-hand side, it is just possible to pick out the tall windows of the former Relief or Boston church, built in 1818, which now houses the local British Legion. At the far end is the Liberal Club, which opened in 1914 and is now the Pheasant Inn.

This postcard, sent in 1930, shows a typical 1920s tourer – possibly a Humber – standing outside No. 19 High Street. At that time these premises comprised two shops: J.C. Clark was a cabinetmaker, upholsterer and undertaker, and also sold china; while next door was John McIvor, the watchmaker, jeweller and optician. In August 1928 McIvor was advertising 'real butterfly wing pictures', including views of the abbey and Queen Mary's House: 'the colours . . . never fade or change with time.' In the 1920s the Spread Eagle Hotel was the headquarters of the Cyclists' Touring Club. It had previously been an important coaching inn, having taken over this lucrative business from the Black Bull in the Canongate. At this time, Alex Harkness at the bottom of the High Street was offering 'cars on hire from sixpence a mile' and 'quick service of petrol from Bowser Kerb Pump'.

Market Place, where five main thoroughfares come together, is the centre of Jedburgh. This photograph was taken from the end of Abbey Place which was formerly the road to Newcastle. The area between the fountain and the pavement on the right of the picture has now been pedestrianised; this area was the site of the Kirkwynd tower which once guarded the approach to the abbey. Between John Sword's and Andrew Telfer's shops – both grocers and wine merchants – Exchange Street (known locally as Burn Wynd) still led to the workhouse at the time of this picture. This gathering may be an agricultural hiring. By 1914 most employment agreements were made privately, but crowds continued to gather in Market Place for the local fairs which continued until after the Second World War. Alternatively, the men may be waiting to hear a visiting speaker – in August 1910, for example, George Kerr of the Hawick ILP (Independent Labour Party) gave a talk on Socialism, arguing for the nationalisation of industry. Although this postcard was sent in 1916, the picture was taken some time previously as James Turnbull's the draper's (right of centre) had made way for R. McIntosh's grocery shop some time between 1910 and 1912. Also in the picture are Walker's Dispensary (which offered a photographic darkroom 'for the use of amateurs'), Hislop and Oliver's drapers and tailors at Albion House, and Scott the baker at 10 High Street.

In the 1930s motor cars were getting faster and popular models such as the Bullnose Morris were bringing the pleasures of motoring to a wider public. By 1935 car parking had become an issue in Jedburgh and reports of motoring accidents and offences were appearing in the local paper. Roxburghshire Police Committee decided it needed a couple of motorcycles to back up the two motor cars it used for speed patrols and bowed to pressure from Edinburgh to co-operate in testing wireless reception in moving police vehicles. Even so, the streets were still quiet enough for people to stand around chatting. Melted tar could be a problem for dogs as well as people, but the *Jedburgh Gazette* had the answer as early as 1928: 'A little butter rubbed into their feet acts as a very effective solvent of tar and is useful for removing any that cannot be reached.' At No. 1 High Street, just behind the postbox, is the jewellers Walter Rule & Sons, a long established business which was already listed at this address in Lamburn's Directory of 1897.

The driver of a large open-top tourer has stopped to change a wheel, watched by a group of children, a youth sitting on the Jubilee Fountain and someone in a window above the Misses Hollands' shop at No. 2 Canongate. The fountain was erected for Queen Victoria's Jubilee. The royal unicorn holds the burgh arms: a rider armed with a Jethart staff. The pipework remains in place, but the fountain is now dry. This picture gives a good view of the Canongate before the buildings at the lower end were torn down. No. 10 Canongate, next to Nobles' grocer shop, was formerly the Black Bull coaching inn. On the corner is the Abbey Temperance Hotel, the ground floor premises of which later became the Mercat Café run by the Massari family. When Mary, Queen of Scots, visited Jedburgh to dispense justice the courthouse was in the 'Tongue' of the Canongate, a row of buildings squeezed into the middle of the street with the Tolbooth at one end and a bakehouse at the other. The Tongue was demolished in the mid-eighteenth century.

Far right: On the right of this picture are the County Buildings which were built in the early nineteenth century by French prisoners of war, on the site of the old Town House. A court room was added in 1861. On the left is the Newgate, built to replace the Tolbooth around the time that the Tongue of the Canongate was demolished. The town steeple was added shortly afterwards. The archway under the steeple leads through to the Ramparts, which still sweep round the eastern boundary of the abbey graveyard as a reminder of the gun emplacements installed by the French in 1548 when they were supporting the Scots against the English. Underneath the archway are a couple of small rooms which may have been used as cells, although the main prison accommodation was upstairs.

Right: No. 26 New Bongate (now renumbered) looks like a mansion but was in reality a tenement of several flats, with the upper storeys reached by a separate entrance. There is no date on this postcard, but at the time of the 1901 census there were five householders here: James Brunton, his wife Joanna and daughters Lizzie and Maggie; Donald and Mary MacPherson and their four sons; Alexander and Mary Dowie and a female boarder; William Henderson, his aunts Margaret and Helen and cousin Margaret Wemyss; and Charles and Margaret Brunton and their four daughters. A long-time resident of New

Bongate was Miss Betty Veitch who died in 1912. Born in 1818, she was the youngest daughter of James Veitch of Inchbonny.

This view of Market Place was taken some time between 1928, when Adam Laidlaw opened his new tearoom, and 1932 when a new plaque was installed on the County Buildings to commemorate Sir Walter Scott's visits to the town as a young lawyer. The signpost shows the A68 to Newcastle and London. The new system of road classification had been introduced after the Ministry of Transport was created in 1919. Signs for 'A' class roads were supposed to be black on white, but local authorities often deviated from the recommendations. Miller's fish shop occupies part of the building where Bonnie Prince Charlie is said to have lodged in 1745 on his way south. The street heading up the hill is the Castlegate, leading to the Dunion hill and eventually to Hawick.

When the Castle Gaol opened for business in 1823 it was considered a model of its type. It had exercise yards and separate blocks for the bridewell (a 'house of correction' which operated under a different regime from the rest of the gaol), for male criminals and for women criminals and debtors. The original Jedburgh Castle stood on the same site and held a commanding position over the town and the abbey. This strategic stronghold was a great advantage to whoever controlled it – but all too often that turned out to be the English. So, in 1409, 'the men of Teviotdale' had it thoroughly demolished at the expense of the Exchequer. In 1886 the gaol was closed and the prisoners were transferred to Edinburgh. The building is now a museum.

When this postcard was sent in 1908 this bridge was on the main route from Edinburgh to Newcastle. On the left is the tower of Jedburgh Abbey, founded as an Augustinian priory by King David I and elevated to abbey status around 1154. During the Wars of Independence the abbey was damaged on four or five occasions and was attacked again during the 'Rough Wooing' of the 1540s by the armies of Henry VIII. The main nave was adapted for use as a parish church, but the congregation moved to the new kirk in 1875. After that bad pointing and frost took their toll, and, in 1913, the building was put into the care of the Ancient Monuments Commission. The building right in the centre of the picture is the Public Hall, built as a replacement for the Corn Exchange which burned down in 1898, taking the town's museum with it. The Public Hall was used for meetings, lectures and Kinema performances. Directly to the left of the Public Hall, almost hidden, is the old Grammar School, built in 1779 and now the Carter's Rest pub. Just past the railings on the far side of the bridge is the southern end of the Ramparts. This spot was chosen for Jedburgh's war memorial and is now a focal point for the town's festival.

This scene from around 1910 shows the other end of the Abbey Bridge, with George Hardie's Allarley engineering works in the centre (now the site of the Kenmore Hall). Even before the Disruption of 1843 Jedburgh was an important centre of religious debate and dissent, and the town had many churches. On the left is the Abbey United Free Church (which no longer stands), behind some empty ground later used to build public baths and a swimming pond, the gift of Mr James Laidlaw of Allars. The new parish church on the right dates from 1875, when the abbey became too dilapidated to be used for services.

In 1935 it was proposed to widen the Abbey Bridge at a cost of well over £5,000. By the time of this view, apparently looking south-west from the vantage point of the abbey tower, the work had been carried out. The striped base on the 'fingerpost' road sign would not have been painted before 1933. The Laidlaw Memorial Baths, built in the early 1920s, are also in place between the laundry and the U.F. church, which was demolished in the early 1970s to make way for a larger pool. Beyond the parish church is the Allerley Well Park and the bandstand gifted by Provost Laidlaw in 1895. The fenced area on the bottom right is now the car park of the Lothian Park.

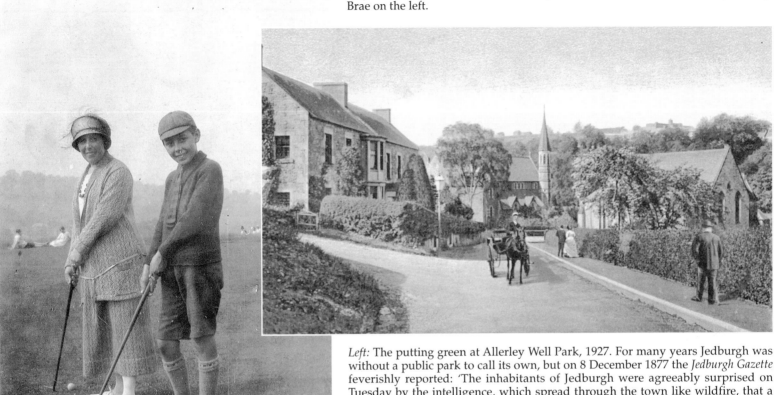

Below: In a scene from well before the First World War, the parish church and the U.F. church are viewed from the north-east along what is now Oxnam Road. The Castle Gaol – disused by this time – is visible on the horizon. The fashionable couple may have been for a turn around Allerley Well Park which can be reached by Allerley Brae on the left.

Left: The putting green at Allerley Well Park, 1927. For many years Jedburgh was without a public park to call its own, but on 8 December 1877 the *Jedburgh Gazette* feverishly reported: 'The inhabitants of Jedburgh were agreeably surprised on Tuesday by the intelligence, which spread through the town like wildfire, that a public park had been purchased as a free gift to the burgh of Jedburgh . . . . Shortly after two o'clock in the afternoon the town's bells began to ring merrily . . . . Some, thinking a fire had broken out, rushed from the workshops and dwelling houses into the street . . .' The donors were the Tinline family, who had bought the Allerley Well field for the purpose. The park was originally to be named Burnet Park after a previous rector of the Grammar School. Before their plans were finalised, the Marquis of Lothian bought the Virgin Glebe and offered it as a recreation ground at a nominal rent. Both parks appear on the 1898 Ordnance Survey map of the town.

Right: A party of merrymakers setting off from outside the Episcopalian Church (the 'English Church') in Friars Road, near the old preaching ground known as the 'Anna'. The tiled roof and wooden supports of the lych-gate are clearly visible. The motor vehicles were built by the Albion Company around 1905 and belonged to Matthew Moore, a local bus operator. The Episcopalian Church did not take part in the United Sunday Schools Picnic, organising its own outings instead. The churchyard contains the tomb of George Tancred of Weens (1831–1914) the author of *Rulewater and its People* and *Annals of a Border Club.*

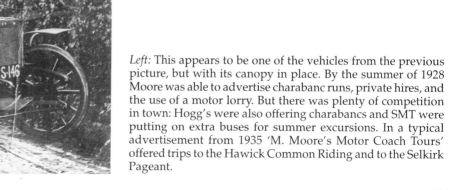

Left: This appears to be one of the vehicles from the previous picture, but with its canopy in place. By the summer of 1928 Moore was able to advertise charabanc runs, private hires, and the use of a motor lorry. But there was plenty of competition in town: Hogg's were also offering charabancs and SMT were putting on extra buses for summer excursions. In a typical advertisement from 1935 'M. Moore's Motor Coach Tours' offered trips to the Hawick Common Riding and to the Selkirk Pageant.

The annual Jedburgh Sheep and Dog Show was held every August in the Lothian Park. Produce such as butter, eggs, honey and homemade scones were judged and there were competitions for collie dogs, greyhounds, and sporting and fancy dogs. The emphasis of the day, however, was firmly on horses and ponies. As well as driving turn-out competitions, there were categories for horses and carts and for 'horse, machine and harness' used by a merchants and tradesmen, as well as pony jumping and pony races. The last show was held in 1938.

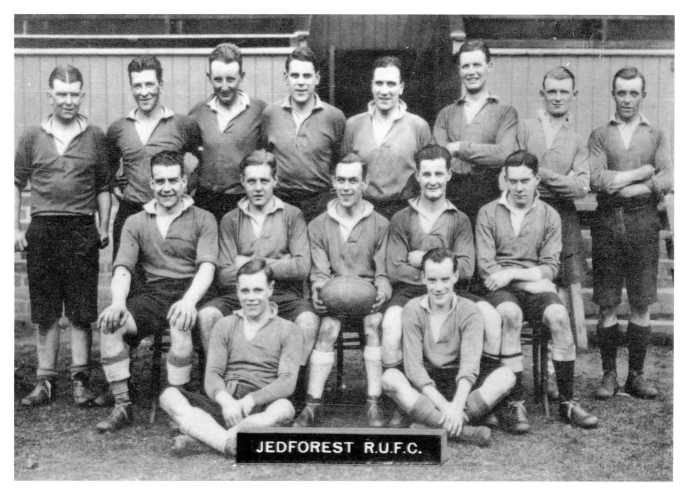

The Jedforest Rugby Club was officially inaugurated in 1885 at a public meeting in the Royal Hotel. This is a classic line-up of players from the 1930s and they are named on the back of this cigarette card. *Back row (left to right)*: W. Purdie, A.N. Other [*sic*], G. Hogg, D. Hastie, G. Blair, W. Wilson, W. Fairbairn, J. Donald; *middle row*: T. Middlemiss, H. Hilson, W. Aitken (Capt.), J. Ewing, A. Stewart; *front row*: J. Jupp, J. Hogg. W. Purdie served as captain for four seasons and capped for Scotland against Wales, Ireland and England in 1939. W. Aitken was captain in the 1931–32 season. Many of the previous generation of Jedforest players were lost in their prime: eighty members of the club joined up for the First World War, including the entire 1913–14 team. The club celebrated its centenary in 1985.

The funeral of William Beaufort Robertson took place on 8 January 1914. Known locally as 'Beauf', he was named after his South African birthplace. His father was a Crimean veteran, serving in the Royal Engineers. Having himself served in the Seaforth Highlanders, 'Beauf' fought in the Boer War as a reservist, losing a leg at Magersfontein in 1899. On his return to Jedburgh he worked as a master shoemaker and was a leading member of the Ancient Order of Foresters, but died from appendicitis at the age of 45. The funeral of this local hero was conducted with full military honours. His sword, cap, belt and sash were carried on his coffin, along with wreaths and a Union flag. This picture shows the closing moments of the ceremony, which were reported in the *Jedburgh Gazette*: 'Three volleys were fired over the grave, a lament being played by the piper between each volley, and at the end the Last Post was sounded by two buglers.'

At the beginning of August 1914, the local MP, Sir John Jardine, spoke in Parliament against the prospect of war, believing that a diplomatic settlement of the Belgium question was still possible. But a couple of days later, on Wednesday 5 August, Army Reserve men left the town by train. At a parade in the Public Hall the same evening, men and boys of the National Reserve were asked to volunteer in order to bring the Jedburgh Territorials up to full strength. On the following Friday morning the Jedburgh Territorials marched from the Armoury in the Castlegate to the railway station. The send-off party shown here included Provost Boyd, Bailie William Oliver and Councillor J.C. Clark. Three cheers were given for the king and the National Anthem was sung. Four more young men – Robert Haig, James Millar, David Rutherford and George Nelson – left on the Saturday and other men of the town volunteered for the King's Own Scottish Borderers Territorials in the Galashiels District. Opened in July 1856, the Jedburgh branch line brought in goods for the shops and shoppers from the surrounding communities. Jedburgh Station, inconveniently situated three-quarters of a mile from the town centre, was closed to passenger traffic after the storms of 1948 and closed to freight in 1964. The site is now taken by an industrial estate.

Local motor drivers and engineers belonging to the Army Service received their orders on Thursday 6 August 1914 and left the same night. They sailed from Liverpool at 3 p.m. on Wednesday 12 August on the steamer *Aquitania* as part of No. 50 Army Service Corps. The men included John Rutherford of New Bongate (engineer), J. Dryburgh, G. Reid, J. Stewart, G. Hogg, W. Freer, John Balfour, G. or A. Telfer (holding cigarette), W. Coltherd, and a man called Butler. Shortly before sailing John Rutherford wrote in a letter: '"Jethart's Here" is a password at the docks . . . . There is a grim determination on the part of everyone to do his bit or die.'

The first Jedburgh Border Games were held to mark the coming of age of the 8th Marquis of Lothian in August 1853. Originally held on the slopes of the Dunion hill, the pre-First World War games took place in the Lothian Park. Contestants arrived by train for the open races which carried prizes of up to £10, with much of the prize money contributed by emigrants living in Canada. Leading citizens and visitors in the grand stand were named in the *Jedburgh Gazette*, which also published full results. Since there is no awning, this photograph probably shows one of the other stands. It was almost certainly taken no later than 1914: the man in the centre next to the two little girls also attended the Oxnam picnic of 1912, and the man with the baby on his knee is among the motor volunteers featured on the previous page. The games now take place at Riverside Park in July to coincide with the Jethart Callants Festival.

Here is Jedburgh in the forefront of 1920s technology. A group of workmen and school children pose beside a motor bus, owned by Brooke and Amos, in front of the Jedburgh telephone 'repeating station'. Dressed in smart uniforms are driver Cairncross Sinton and the conductor who was also named Sinton. 'Cairney' Sinton is still remembered as a bus driver by people in the town today. New in 1925, the Leyland bus's double running boards and rows of doors look strikingly similar to the company's large N-type charabancs which also had wood and metal bodywork. Unlike the charabancs, this vehicle has modern pneumatic tyres. Based in Galashiels, Brooke and Amos were taken over by the Scottish Motor Traction Company Ltd in 1926 and run as a subsidiary of that company until full acquisition in 1928. In June that year the SMT announced an Edinburgh–Jedburgh–Newcastle service with Walter Easton's *Gazette* office as Jedburgh agent. Two doors away in Market Place, Adam Laidlaw was local agent for the M&P Company which offered 'new coaches' and identical fares. One of the Amos family, James, later became general manager of the SMT.

SANGER'S CIRCUS HORSES, "WATERING IN THE JED

Horses of Sanger's circus being watered in the Jed, *c.*1910. The Sangers were one of Britain's most successful Victorian circus dynasties. George and John Sanger were sons of a ploughboy who was supposed to have served under Nelson at Trafalgar and used his pension money to buy a travelling peepshow. George married a lady lion-tamer named Nellie Chapman and the brothers started their circus in the 1850s. The self-styled 'Lord' George later retired, and was murdered in 1911, so this picture is probably of his nephew's circus, John Sangers and Sons, which continued into the 1930s. The circus employed well over a hundred people, including thirty or so grooms to look after the horses, which were used for performances and transportation and for pulling the magnificent tableau parade wagons.

1935 was an important year for the Jedburgh Border Games. This was the first time that the streets were decorated, the first year of the Race Round the Town, and the first year that a pageant was included. This entry by the North British Rayon Company won a prize in the 'Special Category'. The monk and peasants gathering pears were Mr K. McDougal and Misses Margaret McDougall, Mary Mackie, B. Burn, L. Hermiston, and Nan Bathgate (third 'peasant' from the left). On the left, in the '1935' section, Miss Joan Kennedy (later Mrs Russell) appeared dressed entirely in 'art. silk' (artificial silk), surrounded by hanks and pirns of yarn and fabrics. The tableau was staged on one of Mr Burns's lorries, driven by Mr J.W. Lowrie. As the *Jedburgh Gazette* put it: '. . . the sheen of art. silk and the manifold nature of its uses in the making of various beautiful fabrics illustrated that Jedburgh is right in the forefront in the modern textile industry.' The North British Rayon mill stood on the site of the old Lady's Yard pear orchards; it closed in the 1950s.

Right: Monteviot House, the family seat of the Marquis of Lothian (the family name is Kerr), was based around an eighteenth century lodge with extensive nineteenth and twentieth century additions. During the Second World War it was used at a convalescent hospital and during the late 1940s and the 1950s it served as a rest home for the White Friars missionaries. The Kerr family returned to the house in 1961, redesigning the interior and the gardens, which are now open to the public during the summer months.

Left: The interior of the Ferniehurst Castle Hostel. The first Ferniehurst Castle was built by Sir Thomas Kerr, whose father was famous for fighting left-handed. The present building dates mostly from around 1598. In 1549 the castle was recaptured by French and Scots forces from a notoriously cruel English governor. The Scots exacted a bloody revenge and in the Jedburgh Handba' game the ba' is sometimes said to represent the severed head of an Englishman. The Kerrs supported Mary, Queen of Scots, but when they sent a proclamation of loyalty to Jedburgh, their herald was famously made to eat the document by the townspeople. Ferniehurst was empty for many years before being let to the Scottish Youth Hostels Association from 1934 to 1985. During the Second World War it was used as a barracks. After carrying out major restoration work, the Marquis of Lothian retired to Ferniehurst in the 1990s, leaving Monteviot in the care of his son, the Earl of Ancram.

Like the Station Bridge, Inchbonny Bridge is one of the five bridges built in the town during the 1920s. Inchbonny was the home of James Veitch (1771–1838), described by Sir Walter Scott as 'a very remarkable man, a self-taught philosopher, astronomer, and mathematician, and certainly one of the most extraordinary persons I ever knew'. As well as making telescopes and clocks, Veitch was once awarded £100 for inventing a new type of plough. In 1787 James Hutton visited Jedburgh and at Allar's Mill, near Inchbonny, he discovered an 'unconformity' of vertical greywackes which had been folded and then eroded before the newer red sandstone was laid down. In his *Theory of the Earth,* published the following year by the Royal Society of Edinburgh, this finding helped Hutton to demonstrate that rocks were being eroded and renewed over vast expanses of time and that the earth was much more than 6,000 years old – a figure based on a literal interpretation of the Bible.

When Mary, Queen of Scots, arrived in Jedburgh in October 1566, to dispense justice at the old Tolbooth, she would have stayed in one of the best houses, although, despite local legend, it is unlikely to have been this one. After an ill-judged ride across country to visit the wounded Earl of Bothwell at Hermitage Castle, Mary fell sick of a fever and lay close to death for some days. She is said to have used a room in the turret of this house and the bed she slept in was later given to Sir Walter Scott, who kept it at Abbotsford. At the end of the nineteenth century, considerable repairs were undertaken and the thatched roof was replaced with red tiles, but then the house seems to have fallen on hard times. In 1909 Charles Irvine was using the grounds for his business as a seedsman and in 1910 the house itself was advertised for rent for several weeks in succession. During 1928 a bazaar was held to raise money to buy Queen Mary's House – a vase donated for this event by the King and Queen was recently discovered at the Castle Gaol. The house was presented to the burgh and was scheduled as an ancient monument in 1935. A small tree in the garden carries a commemorative plaque which reads: 'Our Queen Mary's Tree, presented by Her Majesty the Queen and planted by Mrs Agnes Well Mabon on site of Pear Tree traditionally known as "Mary Queen of Scots Tree", 29th November 1934.' The tiled roof was replaced with slates in 1980.

OXNAM PICNIC 1912 N°3

For their picnic at the end of July 1912, the children of the district assembled at the Manse where they were welcomed by the Rev. Mr Gunn and his wife. At one o' clock Piper Forbes from Kelso arrived, playing the 'Campbells are Coming', and they all moved off to the picnic field at Oxnam Row – two or three acres of level grass with the green slopes of Row Hill for seating. Such events were given full coverage in the *Jedburgh Gazette*. This picture probably shows the scene later in the afternoon, when parents and friends began to arrive. A 'larger gathering than there has been for some years' was attributed to good weather and the number of visitors staying in the district.

Another picnic scene, perhaps from the same year. In 1912 Mr Jack, the Jedburgh photographer, was present during the afternoon and took 'several views of the most interesting groups'. This one seems to include Piper Forbes and the Rev. Gunn, who later awarded the prizes for regular attendance at Sunday school. At the end of the day there were hearty cheers for all concerned, including Mr and Miss Borthwick who had lent them the field at Oxnam Row farm, and 'for themselves for being good children'.

Guests at the Oxnam picnic are seen here balanced on a see-saw. At the 1912 picnic the games included 'jing-go-ring', Aunt Sally and cricket. The sports included wrestling, lots of races for boys and girls of different ages, thread and needle races, and a 'Married Ladies Race'. Skipping for girls under fourteen was won by Mary Fraser – 200 not out! After the picnic was finished the 'young folks remained and spent an hour or two in sports and dancing, the music of Piper Forbes being a great inducement and much appreciated.'

This view shows the picnic of 1913. Once again it was held at Oxnam Row and Piper Forbes led the procession from the Manse in fine weather. According to the *Gazette*, 'much work in preparing the tea had been done by Mrs Gray, Mrs Hunter, Mrs Duncan, and Miss Chrissie Black, and the beverage they produced was highly spoken of even by some notable connoisseurs who were present'. The tea-making equipment appears to include a Soyer stove, a type used by the army. Those present included the Rev. Gunn, Mrs Gunn, and members of their family and friends; Mr T. Clark, Pleasants School Superintendent; Mr J.D. Little of Oxnam School; Miss Bessie Riddell; Miss Gunn; and Miss Hilda Gunn. The children 'carried a large number of flags. The foremost of them bore the words – Oxnam Sunday School. Of this banner and others the poles were surmounted with flowers and leaves.'

The celebrated divine, Samuel Rutherford, was a key figure in the Covenanting movement. Born at Nisbet in 1600, he was probably educated at Jedburgh before entering Edinburgh University. Rutherford gained his masters degree in 1621 and in 1623 was elected Professor of Humanity. In 1627 he became parish minister at Anwoth in the Stewartry of Kirkcudbright. He was immensely influential and great crowds came to hear him preach, but in 1636 he was deprived of his pastoral charge for non-conformity. Appointed Professor of Divinity at St Andrews' University, and later Rector, he also preached in London. At the Restoration he was deprived of his office and summoned to appear before Parliament. However, he died before he could do so, on 20 March 1661.

In the early years of the twentieth century many of the communities around Jedburgh had an annual show. Ancrum and Crailing had horticultural shows, but Pennymuir had an annual 'horticultural, pastoral and industrial exhibition'. The show still takes place every September and this is one of the past committees of judges. In marked contrast to the Jedburgh Sheep and Dog Show, this was an event for shepherds, with a sheep dog trial, sports, and a stick-dressing competition. The ladies in the picture were there to judge the 'industrial' competitions such as baking and sewing. Regular judges before the First World War included Miss J. Barrie of Harden, T.S. Pearson Esq. of Otterburn (sports) and Charles Irvine, the Jedburgh seedsman (vegetables). The old Roman road passes near Pennymuir on its way to *Trimontium* (Newstead).

Eckford lies near the River Teviot, about halfway between Jedburgh and Kelso. The parish church is some way from the centre of the village and the graveyard has an unusual mort-house where watchers would sit all night, armed with whisky and a flintlock gun. This crossroads is believed to have been the site of a defensive tower burnt by the English in 1544, at the same time as an earlier parish church was razed to the ground and its bell carried off to England. This picture dates from before 1904.

Like many Borders schoolmasters, William G. Sanson served the children of his village, Eckford, for several decades. The young people in the picture may include his own children, Agnes, Kate and Adam. Children who passed the qualifying exam had the chance to go on to the Grammar School at Jedburgh, but most stayed on in the village school and left at the age of fourteen. This school and schoolhouse are now a private dwelling. The long playground leading down to the road is being redeveloped to provide an access road for new houses.

The son of a gardener, George Fargie was teacher at Crailing Public School for forty-one years, assisted by his daughter Mary and a part-time sewing mistress. At the time this picture was taken, the county authorities were greatly concerned about the spread of disease. In May 1910 Dr Oliver, the Medical Officer of Health for Roxburgh County Council, gave his annual report. Of fifty-five schools in the county, 'thirty-two were more or less affected by epidemic disease' and fifteen were closed for varying periods for the same reason. George Fargie retired to Fife a year or two after this picture was taken and died in August 1912 from heart disease.

At the time of this picture, the Rutherfords had been farming at Crailing Tofts for at least fifty years. Walter Rutherford, who had taken over from his father Walter, was a keen golfer, a leading liberal, JP, and a member of the school board and the parish council. Both Crailing Tofts and its cottages lie on a long straight stretch of what is now the A698 to Kelso. On 24 June 1910, the *Jedburgh Gazette* noted that 'Mr Walter Rutherford has been treating the road at Crailing Tofts with a preparation for laying dust. The road dealt with extends from Crailing Tofts farm steading to near Pennymuir road end.' Walter Rutherford died from diabetes in October 1913, leaving one son, also named Walter, although it was his wife who took over the farm.

Walter Rutherford also ran Cessford Farm for a time, after the death of his brother in law; on the Duke of Roxburgh's estate, it remains one of the largest farms in the area. At the time of this photograph the cottages, which are overlooked by the massive walls of Cessford Castle, would have housed a changing population of hinds and bondagers taken on at local hiring fairs. Bondagers were women workers hired as part of a man's contract with the farmer. They did heavy work and wore a distinctive costume with a striped skirt and large straw bonnet. The footbridge near the smithy in the foreground leads over the Cessford Burn. Today, the cottages look much the same, but the smithy is in a ruinous state.

Below: The Rev. John Paton, in his contribution to the *New Statistical Account of Scotland* (1837), described 'various caves [at Ancrum], amounting in all to fifteen, hewn out of the rocky banks of the river in the most inaccessible places.' He believed the caves had been used as hiding places during the border wars. They were difficult to get to and had 'been provided with fireplaces and apertures in the roof to carry off the smoke . . .' 'Thomson's Cave' was supposed to have been used by James Thomson, the author of 'The Seasons' and 'Rule Britannia'. Others were used by the poor and homeless, or played in by local children. This postcard may have been published by Miss Helen Black, who took over Ancrum Post Office from her aunt in 1900.

Left: Only a few stones remain of the Nether Mill at Ancrum, but the Ordnance Survey map of 1863 shows it as a large corn mill lying close to the Ale Bridge, below what is now the A68. In the seventeenth century it was the scene of a dramatic rescue when the Rev. Livingston's wife fell from her horse into the water and local people turned back the mill wheel to free her.

The Upper Mill stands to the north-west of Ancrum, within shouting distance of where the Nether Mill once stood. This idyllic scene is much changed since the draining of the mill lade and the buildings have been turned into private houses. Some of the Ancrum caves are situated in the sandstone cliffs in the background. In the 1890s the Ale and Teviot rivers were both frozen so deeply that the Rev. Baikie of the Free Church succeeded in skating to Hawick and back.

A group of children standing on the western side of Ancrum village green, in front of the lime trees which were presented by the Marquis of Lothian. Their school can be seen in the distance, together with the clock presented to the village in 1885 by John Paton Esq. of New York. This postcard was printed by G.H. Turnbull of Jedburgh around 1916, after he took over Smail's printing business in the town's High Street. The market cross may have stood near here before being moved to its present position on the green. The area shown is now the site of the village war memorial.

As well as the usual childhood games, Ancrum children had their own Ba' Day to look forward to. The adult game started off in front of the Cross Keys Inn and was so rough that householders needed to protect their windows and gardens. Ancrum now has few shops, but a century ago things were very different. Under 'Ancrum and Neighbourhood', Lamburn's Directory of 1897 lists two blacksmiths, two boot and shoemakers, two butchers, two drapers and clothiers, and no fewer than four grocers and general merchants – John Bell, Jane Black, George Temple and George Hogg, who was also the local baker. Both John Buchanan at the Cross Keys and James Galloway at the Commercial Inn offered stabling and there were three market gardeners, three millers, a traction engine proprietor, and two joiners or cartwrights. A couple of names appear more than once. If the villagers and farmers felt dissatisfied with the choice of shops and services, they could catch a train from Jedfoot or walk the two or three miles over the hill to Jedburgh. R.L. Baxter sold his bakery business in January 1914.

In the summer of 1910, an advertisement on behalf of Ancrum Parish Council appeared in the *Jedburgh Gazette*: 'The Council, having accepted management of the Village Green, . . . hereby give notice that no HORSES or COWS WILL BE ALLOWED ON THE GREEN AFTER THIS DATE. Ancrum, 12 August 1910.' This was not the first attempt to control the use of the green, which had been enclosed by a low wall some forty years before, in order to keep off wagons, carts and gypsy caravans. The large shed in the middle distance is still standing, and was probably once a flax-dressing shed.

The Ogilvie family bought the estate of Chesters near Ancrum from the Bennet sisters in 1787, and in 1790 completed a new mansion, using stone from their own quarries in the parish. Thomas Elliott Ogilvie Esq. of Chesters died 'without issue' in 1896 and in the early years of the twentieth century the house was the home of his widow, Mrs Hope Ogilvie, and his nephew Percy. In January 1914, the *Jedburgh Gazette* noted that Mr P.G. Ogilvie of Chesters had given each householder on the farms of Broom, Chesters and Chesters Craig a stone of beef on New Year's Day. The workers were also given holidays on Christmas Day and New Year's Day, and 'Mr Ogilvie's kindness and liberality were much appreciated'.